Contents

Part 1: Introduction *page* 5

A note on the text 8

Part 2: Summaries 9

A general summary 9

Detailed summaries 10

Part 3: Commentary 48

The characters 48

Narrative technique 58

The world of *Vanity Fair* 62

Part 4: Hints for study 68

On writing examinations 68

Questions and answers 69

Scenes for special study 75

Part 5: Suggestions for further reading 76

The author of these notes 78